Time Matters

Julie Anne Gilligan

'We must use time as a tool, not as a crutch'
John F Kennedy

Time Matters
© Julie Anne Gilligan
First Edition 2022
Julie Anne Gilligan has asserted their authorship and given
permission to Dempsey & Windle for these poems to be
published here.
Published by Dempsey & Windle
15 Rosetrees
Guildford
Surrey
GU1 2HS
UK
01483 571164
dempseyandwindle.com
A catalogue record for this book is available
from the British Library
British Library Cataloguing-in-Publication Data
ISBN: 978-1-913329-80-8
Printed and bound in the UK

DEDICATION

Many thanks to all my poetically-inclined friends, especially in OU Poets, in *Poets Abroad* and those who began the OU creative writing journey with me in 2006. Most of all I thank my family, without whose support and encouragement I would have given up writing years ago, or possibly might never have started.

Contents

Some poems included in *Time Matters* have previously been published:

An earlier version of 'The Shipping Forecast is History' in Gilligan JA (2012)' *The Thickness of Blood'* Monkey Business

'Catching Stars' in earier version, as 'A Rare Storm' in First Class: Early Works of the Nearly Famous, ed .G K Talboys 2007 Monkey Business.

The Artist Speaks Across Millennia': in *Nine Muses Poetry* (online)

'Caliban Recast': in *poetsonline* 2021 (Shakespeare character challenge)
,
'No Last Line:' highly commended and published online in *Sentinel Literary Quarterly* ,April 2018.

'Too Young to be Old' was published in translation (M C Gardner 2019) in *ProSaeculum,* a Romanian literary journal.

STORYTIME

Here we are, trapped in the amber of the moment.
There is no why   Kurt Vonnegut

Once upon a time, the dawn of time, everything was timeless.
Yet at another time, time stood still. As time lapsed, Man the
Hunter came along to capture the moment.

As time was, and is, inedible to humans but not, apparently, to
time-consuming activities, Man decided on a timeframe to
freeze-frame time and put it on a pedestal.
Later, finding his sundial somewhat unwieldy and most unsuited
to cave-dwelling, he made clocks in his own image.

He gave them face and hands to count the days, take the minutes
and one just-a-second hand to show it was alive and ticking. But
did time exist before Man caught it, defined it, time-tabled it
with alarming accuracy? Was time self-aware before Man was
time-aware?

Fortunately for time, Woman was made aware, gathering up the
time pieces that Man dropped on his way down the timeline.
Being a designated Gatherer she put them away in a safe place.
Lost time was later found and used up in Time Management
meetings.

Does time know its own up-time and downtime? Tide times and
times tables? Meanwhile back at the horologist's, somewhere in
the space-time continuum, are we an experiment in time,
watched over by the ultimate time-traveller? Who knows?

A stitch in time may save nine but what if the stitch is dropped? Who will restart the race against time? Who will take time to call 'Time Please'? If only time and tide would wait for someone, anyone, will it be the Atomic Clock, the all-powerful definer of time? Given time, it will be accurate for millennia. But who is counting? Who holds the stopwatch?

There is no time like the present, obviously. It was, is, will be forever, the perfect present for someone, somewhere, sometime.

PAST FORWARD

People will not look forward to posterity who never look
backward to their ancestors.   Edmund Burke

I know where they've been,
the people I come from.
My history's no mystery:
the key is, I'm keen
to find all the forebears
who shaped my family tree.
Unravelling the past
makes it clearer to see
how they lived their lives daily
with examples they set
recorded, decoded:
I'll make sense of them yet.
If they knew who their genes made,
how the future might be,
I hope they'd look kindly
to make sense of me.

To make sense of me
I hope they'd look kindly
how the future might be
if they knew who their genes made:
I'll make sense of them yet
recorded, decoded
with examples they set.
How they lived their lives daily
makes it clearer to see.
Unravelling the past,
who shaped my family tree,
to find all the forebears:
the key is, I'm keen.
My history's no mystery:
the people I come from
I know where they've been.

SITTING COMFORTABLY

*The fifties – they seem to have taken place on a sunny afternoon
that asked nothing of you except a drifting belief in the moment
and its power to satisfy.*   Elizabeth Hardwick

Wholesome breakfast set you up for the day: eggs or porridge with
a swirl of golden syrup; Sunday roasts; apple pie, cloves and
cinnamon; Proper custard made with Bird's powder and
evaporated milk; or rice pudding, gold-brown nutmeg-rippled like
tiger fur.

Free milk at school, crates with third of a pint bottles, drunk with
straws. Times tables, Kings and Queens, sums, stories, painting,
clay, hopscotch and tag, skipping ropes, country dancing, Music
and Movement: BBC Schools' programmes.

Most men worked on Saturday mornings. Weekends were shorter
then. Time could not be used lightly. The war was won; get on
with the peace. Tennis and gardening, long walks after Sunday
dinner; trips to the nearest seaside.

Flowers in vases: double dahlias, deep purple, the size of breakfast
bowls, soft as fledglings' feathers. Flamboyant because plants
could again be grown for flowers alone. Dig for Victory was done.
But you could still pick wildflowers then.

Four minutes before the Six O'Clock News, silence fell
unrequested at the altar of the BBC: the wireless was switched on
for the Shipping Forecast. Earlier, there had been 'Listen with
Mother' and 'Woman's Hour'.

TVs were hired on the 'never-never' most acquired for the Coronation. We were mesmerised by the Test Card and the picture shrinking to a tiny point of light, a distant star in infinite blackness of space. Most folk knew nothing of cathode ray tubes or firing electrons. Or space.

The bleach-scrubbed kitchen table, pale as dry bones, was for homework, newspapers, crosswords, jigsaws, sewing new clothes, mending old ones, discussion about history, causes of wars and how they were won. How things will always get better, given time.

A PINCH OF SEASONING

What is beautiful is a joy for all seasons,
a possession for all eternity.   Oscar Wilde

Spring woodland: beech, oak, ash,
lakes of bluebells spill into hedgerows
splashed with ice-white stitchwort.
        Birds collect winter debris
        for their next generation.

Summer meadow: Oxeye daisies, chicory, yarrow,
vetches and trefoils, pale yellow tansies, sun-dried hay.
Clay-on-chalk, unbreakable as over-baked pastry,
        flecked with flint fragments
        that might have been arrow heads.

Autumn harvest: a wooden hay rake draws memories
like crumpled leaves, fallen but still
with the faintest colours of summer.
        Frosted air, misted breath, apple wood fires
        cider-scented, when sleep comes easily.

Winter creeps like a leopard on soft paws,
toys with half-dead dreams and year-end ambitions.
Whatever haze may cloud those days of childhood,
        through mothers' eyes and story times
        the seasons' magic never really ends.

OBSERVING LOCAL CUSTOMS
Inspired by Park By-laws c1930s

The mending of chairs is forbidden
according to Park byelaws imposed by notices
prominently displayed
for the good of the common people.
Respectable persons who took their ease
in a gentle walk, perhaps paused
by the bandstand, listened to a brass ensemble.

Law-abiding people who had not considered
making or mending chairs, dropping litter,
walking on grass (if so instructed).
or *acting in a lewd or inappropriate manner*
or *causing a disturbance*
or *public disorder*
necessitating the *intervention of the Constabulary*
leading to *prosecution of said offender(s).*

Two decades later the park keeper was king
in his brown uniform; brown fedora.
He would materialise, as if at will,
to deter any wrongdoing, breach of regulations
or merely to survey his realm with a glare and a squint
designed to instil in us a respectful fear of authority.

Public conveniences in parks were open at convenient times.
Kept pristine. A place where we learned another fear;
framed notices warning of the perils of venereal disease.
Before we knew anything about anything, we did acquire
a lifelong wariness of toilet seats.

OFF LIMITS

If you don't know where you are going, any road
will get you there. Lewis Carroll

Footpath of sorts, not paved nor level, downhill short cut to bus
stops. Scented with leaf-mould, a quagmire in winter. Snatches of
dense brambles, candyfloss pink willow-herb, 'fireweed'; conker
trees, leaves splayed like hands, reaching out to lean on back
garden fences. Maddie's dad used to rant about small boys, sticks
and stones, conkers dropped on rabbit hutch, veggie plot. Later,
orders came, path forbidden. No reason given. We asked...**no.** Or
The Old House? Hit by incendiaries, burnt down... **No**. But we *did*
climb walls, *did* explore caverns of rubble. The well. We knew
where it was.

We knew it all.

Rats and old mattresses, dog walkers, school kids, men in macs,
footpath closed, play curtailed, plans derailed
no more sense of peace, no timelessness
and now, no conker trees, just
eighteen flats.

SOCKS

*[On being summoned to the Headmistress's study to face
accusations of undermining authority and, over half a century
later, reflecting on how she might have felt about it all...]*

'Don't take that tone with me, girl.
Denial only makes it worse.'
> *Girls like you just make my toes curl*
> *Your bare-faced lies are such a curse.*

> *My last year before retirement, girl.*
> *So what could I do in time that remained?*
> *Admonish? Punish? Let it pass, girl?*
> *No, not that, it would go right against the grain.*
> *I suppose you thought I was out of date,*
> *out of touch...*
> > (I never would have dared)

'Now I'm out of patience. You are wearing the **wrong** stockings!
Non-regulation, the incarnation of disobedience,
all sense of unquestioned discipline, of our great tradition,
guidance set by our forefathers, is lost. Lost, I say'.

> 'But Miss! Miss! I say, again, I'm not!'
'What? What?' The bony finger points...
> 'Not **stockings**, Miss' (I should have said)
> 'Nowadays, these are known as
> **socks...**

1960s c o n c r e t e e v i d e n c e

Some minds are like concrete: thoroughly mixed and
permanently set.'   Anon

monumental galleries.'60s new brutalism
born-again Le Corbusiers
wall to mall containment
kerbs to curb
box girder bridges
Ronan Points
Mies van der Röhe said
'Less is more'
Frank Lloyd Wright's retort
'only where more is no good'
globalised and concretised by-roads
paths and bridges, palms to cross
unlovely urns are made to look
like stone
marbled
sometimes
bunkers and tank traps
roadblocks and barricades
demolish arguments win on aggregate
cement our relationships
concretions built on shored foundations

21ˢᵗ CENTURY FLAT EARTH SOCIETY

The further a society drifts from the truth, the more it will hate
those who speak it.
George Orwell.

We live on a raft
of our own making We live our lives
quietly while all around us things happen
We watch it all move on our flat walls We define
what is real what is truly unbelievable We are sure
we are the centre We fix our own borders We know
when Sun is switched off Moon is lit for our benefit His
pale flat face sometimes smiles We will never surrender
Why should we believe Earth's a ball, circles Sun, and Moon's
pale flat face will never smile We will never surrender
When Sun is switched off Moon is lit for us, our benefit
We are the centre We fix our own borders We know
what is real what is truly unbelievable We are sure
We watch it all move on our flat walls We define
quietly while all around us things happen
of our own making We live our lives
We live on a raft

CATCHING STARS: *Luxor, Egypt, November 2002*

There's a warm wind blowing the stars around.
England Dan and John Ford Coley 1976

Mountains to the west, bleached to a pale gold haze, appeared to fade further as the fertile green border blurred into the water. The south wind prevailed. We were told it would carry a storm from the desert, dust first, rain later, *In sha' Allah*. Illusions of calm disappeared. The timeless feluccas switched stately pavane to slip-stream sashay. They raced to find shelter alongside the dock where the white-sailed gaff-riggers and baksheesh seekers vied with each other for lucrative business.

From our safely moored viewpoint we watched the deluge develop. Rain rattled on rooftops, sounds like shutters pulled down over jewellers' shop windows, well-lit behind. Glimpses of pearls and diamond-flashed droplets, rainbow oiled puddles in streets without drains. Gutters were running with children in ecstasy, springs released, uncoiled in a frenzy: no rain had fallen for more than five years.

Also resting on board, the distinguished old soldier with his smartly dressed lady, stayed cosily closeted in a position of prominence: newspapers poised in post-prandial stupor, their faces like parchment, dried in the wind. He muttered awake for the expected report: 'There was a storm, did you know, while you were asleep?' 'I knew that there would be.' The old warrior smiled. His words knew their places. His eyes closed again.

Onward to evening, when the rains had passed by us, we boarded the bus to the Temple of Luxor: a Son et Lumiere there was not to be missed. We paused between columns, once seamlessly linked, their colours of greatness made wan by the years. The overture was awesome: the performance began. Unseen, unbidden, from beyond the wide river, from the Valley of Kings and the silence of stone, nature's percussion accompanied the concert: rumbles of thunder rolled out dramatic encores.

Sheet lightning flashed frequently, flickering emerald, a natural backdrop to time-honoured tales. The immortality of Kings was surely reasserted. The way that their part most perfectly fitted was a potent performance, an unpackaged privilege. Speechless, we returned to our water-borne comfort. The Nile slapped gently in the calm after storm. Treacle-dark night was shattered by moonlight, as it was for the ancients: the stars will move on.

THE ROMAN SOLDIER DREAMS OF HOME

*The weak have one weapon: the errors of those who think they
are strong.*   Georges Bidault 1962

Helmet: silvered brass, double eagle crowned;
shield boss, gleaming, a likeness of Hercules;
I draw strength from his image.

At the *hippika gymnasia* we reflect the glory
of our Empire, flashes of light, clash of metal,
armour bright as Sol.

My horse magnifies the spectacle, he wears
his *chamron* without fuss, it protects his face.
He knows his good fortune

as I do: few are accepted into the cavalry;
but almost a thousand of us are at *Stanwix,
ala militaria*. Hadrian *Imperator*

designed this wall, directed construction,
now almost complete after fourteen years.
The peasants watch but do not learn;

little wonder they are ruled, never destined
to rule. We trade of course, where else
would we get our horses' feed?

My name is not important, I am but one
decurion; Hadrian's name will live beyond mine.
Yet we who guard this remote outpost

of Empire, this cold damp border,
will not allow the wall to fall,
as Rome itself will never fall.

At home the heat will be soporific,
grapes will ripen, Bacchus willing.
I dream of hot baths, scented with herbs.

FIRST CUT

A lawn is nature under a totalitarian rule' Michael Pollan

New Year starts when I open the shed, pull bolts
top and bottom, stiffened like me by winter.

It is a ritual, opening to release musty scents:
cedar, earth, creosote, paraffin, beeswax.

Like a miniature of the old ironmonger's shop,
he in brown warehouse coat, white hankie in top

pocket, pencils, notebook, a tape around his neck
like a badge of office, like a tailor, or mayor

or how a doctor wears a stethoscope.
I inadvertently disturb a tidy nest of spiders

which explodes from the grass-box: an arachnid diaspora
of tiny golden flecks, watched by their parent

who sits in the corner, glowers and sheds
another skin whilst I make the first cut.

Up and down, side to side, another observance;
a spring genuflection to nature.

THE ARTIST SPEAKS ACROSS MILLENNIA

Inspired by cave painting at Altamira, Spain

It is finished! In time for another Spring,
a new cycle of seasons brings light from darkness.
My eyes are strained from my winter work
with colours I collected at summer's end.

Rich shades of autumn: reds, ochres, umbers,
sienna, earth, sand, pounded, powdered.
Charcoal from wood fires, greys, whites, ash, chalk.
Mixed with oil from animal fat, just enough.

Colours are limited in range but suit my subjects.
I paint animals like prayers, offerings.
A wish for a plentiful year ahead. We who live
our lives in caves must live always in hope.

Food for tomorrow, for our survival.
We eat to live, we live to die.
These paintings need little translation:
they are the hope that we will not be forgotten.

THE CABINET-MAKER'S TOOLCHEST

Tools have their own integrity'　　　Vita Sackville-West

Sold. A chest emptied of memories, once a way of life. To open the lid and handle the tools was to free history, family gatherings: an illusory perfect past. As if the great-aunts still sleep, snoring softly, in their accustomed armchairs. As if uncles still chuckle in corners like they did as children. As if cards are ready for *pontoon* or *rummy*, and cues are in their rack for after-supper *billiards*. As if the wraiths of tobacco smoke still rise to the darkness of the high yellowed ceiling and the acrid taste of coal is still harsh on tongue and nose. As if the oak furniture, formed with those tools was still in its old rightful place. Bees-waxed sideboard, always cake-laden. Whatnots, with their aspidistra sentinels, symmetrical about the bay window, itself lace-netted as decorum dictated. Dresser, with string inlays, glass doors reflecting flickers of light, warmth of fire and family.

That furniture was crafted out of love and home. The art of wood, sculpted, practical. I close the lid, ask forgiveness from my long-dead grandfather; consign to auction. Another future, another past. I accept the loss. I have the cabinets. The maker moves on.

THE SHIPPING FORECAST IS HISTORY

...expected later. Moderate. Good.

Before the news and after tea
We used to listen every night
And thought of those out on the sea

Their names are part of history
Dogger, Fisher, German Bight
Before the news but after tea

Defined by lines not clear to see
How did they know just which was right?
A thought for those out on the sea

Rivers, ports and islands, seas
Humber, Thames and Dover, Wight
Before the news and after tea

Lundy, Fastnet, Irish Sea
Plymouth Sound and Portland Light
For those in peril on the sea

Names worth the cost of license fee
Partly habit, partly rite
Before the news but after tea
Remember those out on the sea

PAST PARTING: Dunwich, Suffolk 1998

To us the ashes of our ancestors are sacred and their resting place
is hallowed ground.   Chief Seattle

Butter yellow gorse susurrates with the plainsong of bees
in tireless pursuit of their eternal mission. Ling and heather
are a blanket of episcopal shades tucked into the backdrop of pines.

Eastwards, the blues of sky and sea are sliced by a kerf of beach,
a triune composition of origin and destiny. The rule of thirds
is observed, an incision strewn with pelagic bric-a-brac.

I stand again at the triangulation station, an obelisk white as innocence,
a trigonometrical fixed point anchored by mathematics while all around
falls away. Each winter storm brings the edge ever closer.

Those remnant cliffs have already dispossessed the sand martins.
Slow and inexorable, the momentum of aeons will claim the ashes of now
scattered with the ashes of before to return them to the source of all life.

There, I saw two red kites rise together from the heather, caught by the wind.
I cried then … as if there was not enough saltwater in the world.
I did come to add, not to take. Except perhaps this tiny posy of heather.
.
It will fade in time, disintegrate. As if it was never needed.
Though I've searched the clear light of Suffolk skies many times,
I saw the kites only the once.

IMMORTAL LINES

Two, four, six, eight, motorway – it's never too late.

Tom Robinson 1978

Continuing this ageing thing is no fair deal:
immortal life is not the norm, diseases may not heal
but degenerate longevity has little to appeal.

Some seek to be immortalised in song or witty ditty:
certainly much easier than living to infinity.
Continuing this ageing thing is no fair deal.

We surely want to foster what we're leaving to posterity
but check the small print thoroughly; make sure the deal is free
of degenerate longevity, it'll never have appeal

With senses most forgotten, memory decreasing,
a thousand years of wrinkles, stop the mirrors from revealing
that continuing this ageing thing is no fair deal

Some peoples say to elongate our time and year's totality
we must maintain a calm outlook, a life without frivolity
but laughter-free longevity has never had appeal.

What I think some really want is not immortal life
as even for Methuselah, three hundred years sufficed
but continuing this ageing thing is no fair deal.

Eternal youth is more in vogue: it's so much more attractive,
but have a care for what you wish in case it really happens
and degenerate longevity has so much less appeal.

'What do we want?' they say, as if they didn't know.
'Immortal life is what we want and we want it now.'
Continuing this ageing thing is no fair deal
but laughter-free longevity has little to appeal.

[27]

TOO YOUNG TO BE OLD

Wrinkles will only go where the smiles have been,
Jimmy Buffet

It's a long way off

When you're young and ready, steady, go for a fast pace
race through life. You're on course, on a heading, no thoughts
of a wedding; fighting for a cause is a cause in itself.

It's a long way off

When you think over forty is over the hill and the state
of the world is the fault of the old, you'll be making plans
for our carers and nursing. Do bear in mind we'll be kicking
and cursing, in return for the years of minding and mending
your grazed knees and fears and mopping up tears.

It's a long way off

One day you'll remember when it's your turn to cry.
It's so hard to be told you're getting too old,
too old to be young, but much, much too young to be old.

It's still a long way off.

ONLY A MATTER OF TIME

Ah, you don't believe we're on the eve of destruction.

1965 Barry McGuire

Imagine the time, the end of time:
no clocks to watch, no watches to clock.
No reason, no rhyme, no more deadlines.

No time elapsed, no parking fines:
go back to sleep, just count the flock.
Imagine the time, the end of time.

No times, no dates, no limiting signs:
no birthday parties, nor Christmas socks.
No reason, no rhyme, or missed deadlines.

According to natural, old designs:
wake up to the light with the crowing cock.
Imagine that time, the end of time.

If it so happens the Creator resigns
in whatever belief there'll be those who mock:
no reason to rhyme with false deadlines.

Apocalypse riders will swoop at a time
when no-one expects; a terrible shock.
Imagine the time, the end of time:
no reason nor rhyme, just one, dead, line.

CALIBAN RE-CAST

Hell is empty and all the devils are here

The Tempest, Wm Shakespeare

My name's the same,
an unchanged Caliban.
A dark soul, half man
half spell-bound and deformed.
You taught me language
thought me the fool
but I learned to curse
the cruelty of your rule.
I curse again the chains
of sorcery that bind me still
in ancient strands of slavery.
You came and set yourself
a king, you ruled my world
with iron hands as you
bind me still with painful bands.
More are coming as you did
in search of respite, peace and rest.
These migrants, weary refugees
paid their dues and bartered lives
to grubby fists and squalid lies
to try to reach my island realm:
if they survive the tempest hell
of storm-plagued ice-cold seas.
Has nothing changed
in these centuries?

ALL TIMED OUT

There are no secrets that time does not reveal Jean Racine

There's always something to regret
when older, wiser we become.
Some things are best to leave unsaid.

We can choose what's left behind.
Some things others should not find.
There's always something to regret.

The sort of things that come to mind
are unsent letters, left unsigned.
Some things are best to leave unsaid.

What point is there to raise old wounds?
Hurting others would seem unkind,
there's always something to regret.

Keep silence, always diplomatic:
take care with what your mind confines,
some things are best to leave unsaid.

Remember all the things you claimed
then bit your tongue, apologised
There's always something to regret
Some things are best to leave unsaid

POLARISING

Smile, breathe and go slowly.   Thich Nhat Hanh

What can I say
when I hurt inside,
when bodily pain
drains into my mind?
I convince myself
that I've really tried
to be and to act
with a certain kind
of positive attitude
with an outlook bright
but sometimes it's hard
to burrow and find
the means and time
to put up a fight
when a grey day
follows a restless night.

When did this happen?
I don't ask 'Why?'
It will follow some pattern,
a plan from on high.
I can't say how I feel;
that's like giving in
and I can't do that,
can't let it win.
I'm positive that
I'll beat it yet,
not to find a cure
except in my head:
where it's basically at.
I have to keep going
in my positive hat.

GULLS CRY

Freedom can be forgotten in repressive countries. To remember
freedom, it will be enough to watch a happy seagull
flying in the sky   Mehmet Murat ildan

Gulls cry
> for lost fish
> for lost souls

Gulls cry
> pity the poor
> pity the rich
> neither knowing the grief
> of the other

Gulls cries
> sear through skies
> laden with promise
> leaden with portent

Gulls cry
> because they can
> because they must

Gulls cry
> someone must
> surely cry for us

NO LAST LINE New York City, Christmas 2000

I can only do two things for them- describe this flight and not add a last line. from 'Photograph from September 11' by Wislawa Szymborska, translated by Stanislaw Baranczar and Clare Cavanagh

From Times Square we stepped down arrow straight sidewalks, tap-tapping our feet to that old Broadway magic, through Madison Square to Lower Manhattan. Stopped by the sea wall at Battery Park, saw the Staten Island Ferry slice through the iced water, cutting wakes spliced to bow-waves that criss-crossed the channels.

Just visible through layers of chiffon-scarf mist, Liberty's torch still held out her promise; the certainty of freedom and comfort for all. Ellis Island lay low, dark in the water, first taste of America for so many long dead. This, their safe haven where all would be welcome, away from oppression, starvation or worse. Their currency was labour, bartered for freedom; worked hard for themselves and their New World order, turned into proud citizens for generations to come. They constructed foundations for those who came later, who built the twin glories of splendour and wealth.

As the last hazy sun slipped below the horizon, the diamond-bright city turned on its night lights. The star-spangled sky turned a deep speckled turquoise, clouds of our breath told of the coldness of night. The bone-biting wind off the sea made us shiver. We turned from the water, thoughts set on warmth.

That district's the hub of museums, memorials: veterans and mariners; the dead of all wars, the American Indian, the Irish connection, the long Jewish heritage, snapshots of history, of what went before.

They stood like sentinels of pain and experience, unknowingly circling a conflict to come. Within the year, New York would be mourning. Whatever the future the past is always present: there is no last line.

AT THE END OF THE DAY

*'Evenings are the beautiful sweet spot between the harsh light
of the day and the dead darkness of night.'*　　　　Anon.

day drips to dusk in high hot summer
sky streaked boldly in paint-box colours
turquoise viridian indigo crimson
raising the moon as a gold doubloon

sky streaked boldly in paint-box colours
vanilla slice clouds meld streaks like furrows
raising the moon as a gold doubloon
barely cools a degree in a light night breeze

vanilla slice clouds melding streaks like furrows
indulgent extravagance of night-scented flowers
barely cools a degree in a light night breeze
until day turns to dusk with autumnal frosting

indulgent extravagance of night-scented flowers
buried in memory under fallen leaf carpets
when day turns to dusk in rime-edged autumn
haze gathers slowly to rise in the valley

buried in memory under fallen leaf carpets
the sky gains the purity of glacial ice
haze gathers slowly to slide down the valley
promising nothing but cold winter weather

the sky gains the purity of glacial ice
its edges marked purple, no summer colour
promising nothing but long cold winter
sleep under cover 'til days grow longer

with edges of purple, no summer colour
through pallor of sleep, spring stands to attention
has slept under cover 'til daylight's longer
the cycle of seasons repeats its connections

through pallor of sleep, spring stirs into motion
soon day drips to dusk in high hot summer
the cycle of seasons repeats its connections
in turquoise viridian indigo crimson

NOW, WHERE WAS I?

Forever is composed of nows   Emily Dickinson

The older I get
the more I forget
details of day to day.

I arrive in a room
forgetting too soon
exactly the reason I came.

My recall power
grows less by the hour
past years have flown away

But say an '80s September?
I'm sure to remember
the weather, the date and the day

Life seems to rush by
though I do *kind of* try
to slow things running away

If I add up the years
it would push me to tears
thinking time's wasted away

What was I saying?
I think I was praying.
Just let me live for today.

'In the new year, never forget to thank your past years because
they enabled you to reach today' Mehmet Murat ildan

JULIE ANNE GILLIGAN

Julie Anne Gilligan's early years were spent in south-east London, close to the Kentish countryside, and she has lived in semi-rural Essex for the past 35 years.

She was brought up on a literary diet of Greek myths, Shakespeare, Lear and Carroll, *The Eagle*, The Goon Show and an alliterative spattering of Keats, Kipling and Coleridge. In spite of all that, she only started writing poetry in 2004. Since then her poems have appeared in several anthologies (including *The Pre-Raphaelite Society*, *Hedgehog Press*, *Culture Matters*, and *The Gibberd Garden*); in e-zines, including *Nine Muses* and *Poets Online*; and in journals (including translations in the Romanian Literary journals *Banchetul* and *ProSaeculum*). Her debut collection *The Thickness of Blood* was published in 2012. In recent competitions she was awarded 2nd Prize by Sentinel Literary Quarterly for '*View from Dystopia*' and commended for '*Not Going Under*' in 'Parkinson's Arts' 2021 competition.

She holds several qualifications, most recently The Open University MA in Creative Writing.(2018).

She is Activities Officer for The Open University Poetry Society and a member of *Poets Abroad*, a collective of poets mostly from Ireland, UK, USA and Australia.

She firmly believes in a positive outlook and a strong sense of the ridiculous, a point of view developed over 24 years of living with Parkinson's.